BISMARCK
AND HOOD

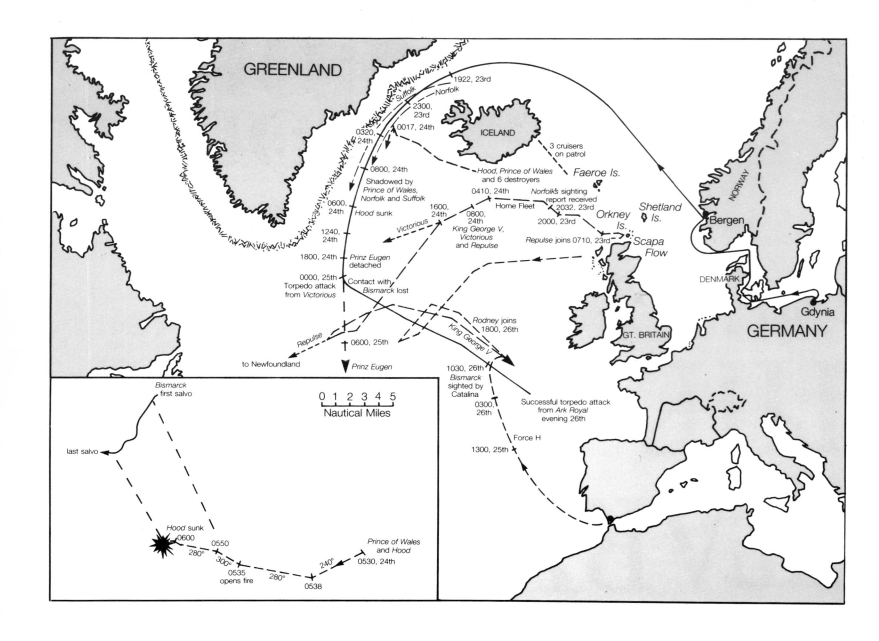

GREENLAND

1922, 23rd

Suffolk
Norfolk

2300,
23rd

0320,
24th   0017, 24th

ICELAND

3 cruisers
on patrol

0800, 24th

Shadowed by
Prince of Wales,
Norfolk and Suffolk

Hood, Prince of Wales
and 6 destroyers   Faeroe Is.

0410, 24th   Norfolk's sighting
report received
2032, 23rd

0600,
24th
Hood sunk

Home Fleet

Shetland
Is.

0800,
24th
King George V,
Victorious
and Repulse

Orkney
Is.

2000, 23rd

Bergen

NORWAY

1600,
24th

Victorious

1240,
24th

Repulse joins 0710, 23rd

Scapa
Flow

1800, 24th   Prinz Eugen
detached

0000, 25th
Torpedo attack
from Victorious

Contact with
Bismarck lost

DENMARK

Repulse

0600, 25th

Rodney joins
1800, 26th

GT. BRITAIN

Gdynia

to Newfoundland   Prinz Eugen

King George V

GERMANY

Bismarck
first salvo

0   1   2   3   4   5

Nautical Miles

1030, 26th
Bismarck
sighted by
Catalina

0300,
26th

Successful torpedo attack
from Ark Royal
evening 26th

last salvo

Hood sunk
0600   0550

Force H

Prince of Wales
and Hood

1300, 25th

280°
300°

0535
opens fire

0538

280°

240°   0530, 24th

BISMARCK AND HOOD

Great Naval Adversaries

PAUL J. KEMP

ARMS AND
ARMOUR

Arms and Armour Press
A Cassell Imprint
Villiers House, 41-47 Strand, London WC2N 5JE.

Distributed in the USA by Sterling Publishing Co. Inc., 387 Park Avenue South, New York, NY 100168810.

Distributed in Australia by Capricorn Link (Australia) Pty. Ltd, P.O. Box 665, Lane Cove, New South Wales 2066.

British Library Cataloguing in Publication Data
Kemp, Paul
Bismarck and Hood: great naval adversaries
1. Great Britain. Germany. Warships, history
I. Title
259.3252
ISBN 1-85409-099-2

Designed and edited by DAG Publications Ltd. Designed by David Gibbons; edited by Michael Boxall; layout by Anthony A. Evans; typeset by Ronset Typesetters, Darwen, Lancashire; camerawork by M&E Reproductions, North Fambridge, Essex; cover illustrations colour simulation by Robert A. Phasey; printed and bound in Great Britain by The Bath Press, Avon.

CONTENTS

BISMARCK AND HOOD

From 24 until 27 May 1941 the attention of the world was focused on an area in the North Atlantic where one of the greatest duels in naval history was being fought to a conclusion. The protagonists were the British battlecruiser HMS *Hood*, a ship which for the twenty-one years of her service life had come to epitomize the power and strength of the Royal Navy, and the German battleship *Bismarck*, a brand-new ship fresh from the builder's yard. On 24 May *Bismarck* stunned the world by sinking *Hood* in a gun engagement that lasted less than ten minutes. Three days later *Bismarck* was herself sunk — battered into a defenceless wreck by the guns of the Home Fleet after one of the longest and most dramatic naval battles in history.

THE SHIPS

HMS *Hood*: Design History

In November 1915 the Admiralty Board called for a design for an experimental battleship with the lightest practicable draught but incorporating the latest ideas in underwater protection. The basis for the design was to be the '*Queen Elizabeth*'-class battleship, but was recast as a 32-knot battlecruiser with 8in belt armour when Admiral Sir John Jellicoe said that such ships would be more useful than 30-knot battleships. However, after the loss of three British battlecruisers during the Battle of Jutland (31 May 1916 – ironically the day the first of the new ships was laid down) work was suspended while the design was reinvestigated. By August 1916 the design was resubmitted as a 37,500-ton ship with a deeper armour belt. However, the Director of Naval Construction proposed a series of modifications which raised displacement to 40,600 tons. In February 1917 the War Cabinet decided that only *Hood* of the four ships ordered should be completed, since there was no evidence that the Germans were completing their capital ship programme. The debate over *Hood*'s construction continued as the various post-Jutland committees submitted their evidence and the final legend (see data section) was not agreed until August 1917. In the final design the Admiralty got what they had originally asked for: a bigger and faster '*Queen Elizabeth*'-class battleship.

The Vexed Question of *Hood*'s Protection

In terms of her armour protection *Hood* represented the ultimate development of the classic British system. A combination of oil fuel tanks and crush-tube spaces gave ample protection against a torpedo hit and introduced a large amount of internal protection against splinters produced by armour-piercing shells burst by the relatively thin side armour – necessarily thin because of the requirement for a high speed. However, her deck protection reflected pre-Jutland thinking and was certainly inadequate against plunging shellfire at long ranges.

While the ship was under construction, considerable concern was expressed over *Hood*'s armour protection, particularly the protection of her decks against plunging shellfire. As a result, further additions were made to her deck protection. In August 1918 approval was given to double the protection over the magazine crowns to 2in by fitting extra 1in plates; weight compensation was found by omitting the 1in and 2in splinter protection to the funnel uptakes above the forecastle deck. In May 1919 an increase in the thickness of the flats above the slope of the main deck around the magazines was also approved; compensation for the additional 100 tons was found by removing four 5.5in gun mountings and their dredger hoists. Finally, in July 1919 approval was given for the increase in thickness of the main deck over the magazines to 6in aft and 5in forward, but this work was never carried out. However, four of the eight above-water 21in torpedo tubes were removed in anticipation of this alteration, which saved some 440 tons of weight. Despite these efforts to save weight, an inclination of *Hood* at Rosyth on 21 February 1920 showed her to have a load displacement of 42,670 tons – 1,470 tons above legend.

As completed, the protection scheme gave *Hood* an Immune Zone – defined as the area from the enemy ship inside which penetration of the belt armour may occur, and outside which penetration of deck armour is possible – of 7,000 yards. At ranges of less than 22,500 yards, penetration of the belt might occur, while at ranges in excess of

29,500 yards penetration of the deck armour by plunging shellfire is possible. Thus, to remain immune from shell fire, *Hood* would be best situated if she engaged her enemy at ranges between 22,500 and 29,500 yards. The 7,000-yard Immune Zone was not wide, thus limiting a commander's freedom to manoeuvre the ship to best advantage, and did not compare favourably with other foreign capital ship designs.

It was recognized in the Royal Navy that *Hood* was deficient in deck protection and that the additions to her protection discussed above had done no more than remedy the worst defects. But she was not a bad design. Her protection was equal to that of the 'Queen Elizabeth' class, but because she was a much larger ship, it was spread over a larger hull. Plans certainly existed to improve her deck protection but they were never carried out due to the lack of funds in the inter-war period and the fact that *Hood* was a relatively new vessel. Her defects were never known outside the Royal Navy. To the general public who equated size with power, she was always 'The Mighty *Hood*'. As discussed in the historical essay, the adequacy or otherwise of *Hood*'s protection was probably not a factor in her loss, but rather, as Admiral of the Fleet Lord Chatfield wrote in *The Times*, that 'she had to fight a ship twenty-two years younger than herself'.

HMS *Hood*: Service History

Date	Event
1 September 1916	Laid down
22 August 1918	Launched
January 1920	Transferred to Rosyth for completion and trials
14 May 1920	Inspected at Rosyth
15 May 1920	Commissioned into the Royal Navy under the command of Captain Wilfrid Tomkinson, RN
15 May 1920–November 1923	Flagship of the Battlecruiser Squadron, Atlantic Fleet
27 November 1923–29 September 1924	Flagship of the Special Service Squadron for a circumnavigation of the world in company with *Repulse* and the First Light Cruiser Squadron to improve Commonwealth relations
January 1925–January 1928	Flagship of the Battlecruiser Squadron, Atlantic Fleet
January 1928–May 1929	Battlecruiser Squadron, Atlantic Squadron
17 May 1929–12 May 1931	Major refit at Portsmouth
12 May 1931–September 1936	Flagship of the Battlecruiser Squadron, Home Fleet. 15 September 1931 *Hood*'s ship's company mutiny at Invergordon after cuts in pay are announced. 23 January 1935 in collision with HMS *Renown*
8 September 1936–January 1939	Mediterranean Fleet
February–August 1939	Refit at Portsmouth
13 August 1939–March 1940	Flagship of the Battlecruiser Squadron, Home Fleet
March – May 1940	Flagship 'Force H' based at Gibraltar. 3 July 1940 attacks French Fleet at Oran
August 1940–May 1941	Flagship of the Battlecruiser Squadron, Home Fleet
24 May 1941	Sunk in action with the German battleship *Bismarck* in the Denmark Strait with the loss of all but three of her ship's company of 1,419

KM *Bismarck*: Design History

Bismarck, with her sister ship *Tirpitz*, were the first proper battleships to be built by the Germans since the Versailles Treaty placed quantitative and qualitative restrictions on German warship construction. Design work began in 1932 but it was not until after the 1935 Anglo-German Naval Agreement that construction began in earnest. Under the terms of this agreement Germany was allowed to build up to 35 per cent of Britain's total tonnage, which meant that she was allowed a maximum battleship tonnage of 183,750. After the three 'pocket battleships' and the two ships of the 'Scharnhorst' class had been built, Germany had a balance of 101,750 tons for capital ship construction. In line with treaties already in force, their displacement was given as 35,000 tons although their true displacement was nearer 45,000 tons. Battleship 'F', later named *Bismarck*, was ordered in 1935 and her sister, Battleship 'G', in 1936. *Bismarck* cost, at 1938 values, RM.196.8 million.

Initially, her design reflected the views of Admiral Erich Raeder, Commander-in-Chief of the German Navy, that the Kriegsmarine should pursue an active strategy of commerce raiding against England, rather than attempt to build up a huge battlefleet which would do little more than swing round a buoy as the High Seas Fleet had done in the First World War. However, during the 1938 Munich Crisis, the German Navy realized that Hitler believed that a war with England was a real possibility. Hitler was not so much interested in battleships as commerce raiders but saw them more as a means of backing up his foreign policy. Accordingly, Hitler ordered a dramatic increase in German naval strength, the well-known 'Z Plan' – and ordered that *Bismarck* and *Tirpitz* be finished ahead of schedule.

KM *Bismarck*: Service History

Date	Event
1 July 1936	Laid down at Blohm und Voss's Hamburg Yard
14 February 1939	Launched
24 August 1940	Commissioned under the command of Kapitän zur See Ernst Lindemann
August 1940–May 1941	Work-up at Gotenhafen (Gdynia) with one final visit to Blohm und Voss for final A & As
18 May 1941	Sails from Gotenhafen with *Prinz Eugen* for Operation 'Rheinübung'
24 May 1941	Sinks HMS *Hood* in action in Denmark Strait. Damaged by 14in hits from HMS *Prince of Wales*. 'Rheinübung' abandoned in favour of making for a French port for repairs
26 May 1941	Disabled by torpedo from Swordfish aircraft launched by HMS *Ark Royal*. During the night of 26/27 May attacked by British destroyers, but sustained no damage
27 May 1941	Battered into a defence-less wreck by gunfire from HM Ships *Rodney* and *King George V* before being sunk by torpedoes fired by HMS *Dorsetshire*. There were 115 survivors out of her ship's company of 2,092 officers and men
1989	Wreck of *Bismarck* located and filmed in the North Atlantic

THE ACTION

German Plans for Commerce Raiding: Operation 'Rheinübung'

The cancellation of plans for the invasion of England in the autumn of 1940 left the German Navy free to concentrate on what it regarded as its main task: the destruction of British commerce in the North Atlantic. Admiral Erich Raeder, C-in-C of the Kriegsmarine, regarded the early cruises of *Admiral Graf Spee* (despite her eventual ignominious end in the muddy waters of Montevideo Harbour) and *Admiral Scheer* as extremely successful. These early cruises were followed by Operation 'Berlin', a cruise by the battlecruisers *Scharnhorst* and *Gneisenau* under the command of Vice-Admiral Gunther Lutjens from January to March 1941 in which twenty-two ships totalling 115,622 tons were captured or sunk.

The success of 'Berlin' had been marred by one factor. The Royal Navy had begun to provide convoys with a capital ship escort, usually one of the older 'Royal Sovereign'-class battleships, which had prevented Lutjens from making the most of his opportunities. But with the completion of *Bismarck*, armed with eight 15in (38cm) guns, and her equally powerful sister ship *Tirpitz*, Raeder had two ships which were more than a match for a British battleship. Raeder could therefore reopen the commerce war by surface ships in the North Atlantic with renewed confidence. Such was the genesis of Operation 'Rheinübung' (Rhine Crossing).

Raeder based his plan on the assumption that both new battleships, *Bismarck* and *Tirpitz*, would be ready together. One could deal with the escort while the other swept up the merchant ships. Unfortunately, due to the Kriegsmarine's insistence on a rigorous work-up schedule of almost peacetime standards, *Tirpitz* would not be ready in time. Instead, the cruiser *Prinz Eugen* (Kapitän zur See Helmuth Brinkmann) was selected as *Bismarck*'s partner. Once in the Atlantic, the two ships would be joined by *Scharnhorst* and *Gneisenau*, which would break out from Brest. However, *Scharnhorst* developed machinery problems while *Gneisenau* was damaged by torpedo on 6 April 1941. *Bismarck* and *Prinz Eugen* would have to conduct 'Rheinübung' on their own.

'Rheinübung': Early Moves

On 19 May 1941 *Bismarck* and *Prinz Eugen* left Gotenhafen on the German-occupied Baltic coast where they had been waiting ever since completing their work-up. They proceeded across the Baltic and by 20 May had cleared the boom at Kristiansund and were heading north. However, the seeds of the eventual failure of 'Rheinübung' had already been sown, for the departure of the German ships had been reported by the Swedish cruiser *Gotland*. Pro-British Swedish naval officers saw to it that this most useful information reached the British Naval Attaché, who passed it to London. An air search of the North Sea between Trondheim and the Naze was ordered but to no avail. It was not until 21 May, during an RAF reconnaissance flight, when Flying Officer Michael Suckling photographed *Bismarck* lying in Grimstadtfjord, where Lutjens had stopped to fuel, that definite proof of *Bismarck*'s departure was received. A strike by RAF Beauforts and Hampdens was ordered but by then the ships had sailed. The next day, 22 May, Commander G. A. Rutherford and Lieutenant N. E. Goddard carried out a perilous low-level reconnaissance of the Bergen fiords in a Fleet Air Arm Maryland and established that the German ships had left. 'Rheinübung' was under way.

British Response

The Home Fleet, under the command of Admiral Sir John Tovey, was quick to respond to the German sortie. The blockade forces in the North Atlantic – comprising the cruisers *Suffolk* (Captain R. M. Ellis) and *Norfolk* (Captain A. J. L. Phillips – flag Rear Admiral W. Wake-Walker) in the Denmark Strait and *Arethusa*, *Manchester* and *Birmingham* in the Iceland/Faroes gap – were ordered to be extra vigilant. The battlecruiser *Hood* (Captain R. Kerr) with the new battleship *Prince of Wales* (Captain J. C. Leach) and six destroyers, under the command of Vice-Admiral Lancelot Holland, were ordered to Iceland to cover the Denmark Strait patrols; while Tovey sailed on 22 May with the battleship *King George V* (Captain W. R. Patterson – flagship), the aircraft-carrier *Victorious* (Captain H. C. Bovell), four cruisers and seven destroyers to cover the routes into the Atlantic south of 62°. At sea Tovey would be joined by the battleship *Rodney* (Captain F. Dalrymple-Hamilton) which had been detached from escorting the liner *Britannic*. Tovey hoped that *Victorious*'s air group, although not properly worked up, would be of assistance in locating *Bismarck*, but bad weather prevented flying operations.

From Gibraltar came the three ships of 'Force H' under the command of the redoubtable Vice-Admiral Sir James Somerville: the battlecruiser *Renown* (Captain R. McGrigor), aircraft-carrier *Ark Royal* (Captain L. Maund) and cruiser *Sheffield* (Captain C. Larcom). 'Force H' was ordered to cover the big convoy WS.8B, but Somerville's ships would soon be playing a critical role in events. At the time the Admiralty's order arrived, 0050 on 24 May, Somerville's ships were at Gibraltar with most of their companies ashore. Nevertheless, by 0305 the ships were clearing Algeciras Bay at 25 knots.

Despite the disposition of his vastly superior forces, Tovey still had no idea of where *Bismarck* would appear. The situation looked grim until 1923 on 23 May when the cruiser *Norfolk* reported that *Bismarck* had been sighted in the Denmark Strait.

Break-out into the Atlantic

The break-out into the Atlantic through the British blockade was the most dangerous part of the operation. Lutjens decided to use the Denmark Strait route rather than the Iceland-Faroes gap which was the route favoured by the German naval high command. Since none of Lutjens' staff or *Bismarck*'s senior officers survived, his reasoning for taking this route, or indeed for any of his other decisions during the operation, must always be a matter for conjecture.

Just after 1922 on 23 May, *Bismarck* went to action stations, having detected a ship using her radar and passive hydrophones. Visual sighting confirmed the ship as a three-funnelled 'County'-class cruiser (in fact, *Suffolk*). *Bismarck* fired a few salvoes of 38cm at the cruiser which retreated into the mist while sending out the first of a series of contact reports; these reports were monitored by the B-Dienst (signals intelligence and code-breakers) teams in both German ships. Roughly an hour later a second cruiser was detected – HMS *Norfolk*.

Action in the Denmark Strait

Once Holland had received the sighting reports from *Norfolk* and *Suffolk*, he realized that he would be in a favourable position to engage the two German ships shortly after daybreak on 24 May. But during the night of the 23rd/24th the cruisers lost contact with *Bismarck* for a period of nearly three hours. Holland believed, wrongly, that Lutjens had given his shadowers the slip by altering course to the south-east. Accordingly he altered course from north-west to north to cut them off. By 0247 on 24 May, *Suffolk* was back in contact with *Bismarck* and Holland swung his ships back to a NW course. However, Holland's manoeuvres during the night had the unfortunate effect of causing him to lose bearing on the enemy.

By 0400 the German ships were estimated to be some 20 miles to the NW of *Hood* and by 0535 *Bismarck* was sighted by *Prince of Wales* at a range of 17 miles off her starboard bow. At 0537 *Prince of Wales* took station on *Hood*'s starboard quarter and both ships altered course to starboard so that they were approaching *Bismarck* practically head-on. This decision of Holland's has earned him the most savage criticism from historians, but in reality there was very little he could do. At the range at which *Bismarck* was sighted *Hood* was very vulnerable to plunging shellfire. It was imperative to close the range so that if *Hood* were hit, it should strike her well protected sides rather than her thinly protected decks. Correct though Holland's thinking was, his decision gave the tactical advantage to Lutjens in that the German ships could pass ahead, crossing Holland's 'T' while committing him to a stern chase instead of being able to cut them off. Furthermore, in approaching the enemy head-on Holland denied his ships the use of their after turrets – almost half his armament – since they would not bear.

Hood was the first to open fire, at 0552 at a range of 25,000 yards, with *Bismarck*'s first salvo following shortly afterwards. Holland had ordered fire to be concentrated on the leading German ship assuming that *Bismarck* would be in the lead. However, after the damage to *Bismarck*'s radar sustained when firing on *Norfolk*, Lutjens had ordered *Prinz Eugen* to go ahead. The mistake was realized by the British, but it is not known whether fire was corrected before *Hood* blew up. Gunnery conditions were not ideal: the speed at which the British ships were travelling meant that spray was sheeting over their bows, making accurate ranging difficult. *Prince of Wales* was fitted with Type 284 gunnery radar but was forbidden to use it by Holland since its transmissions might be picked up by the Germans.

On the other hand, *Bismarck* was shooting superbly, aided no doubt by her excellent stereoscopic rangefinders. *Bismarck*'s first salvo fell short, the second over, the third was a straddle, while the fourth was a close short. *Prinz Eugen* was also shooting well and an 8in (20.3cm) shell from her second salvo struck *Hood* on the boat deck by the mainmast, causing a fierce fire among the ready-use 4in ammunition and URP rockets stowed there.

At 0555 Holland ordered the first of two turns to port which would open his 'A' arcs and allow him to bring the after turrets of his ships to bear. At 0600 *Hood* had the second '2 Blue' pendant flying but before it was hauled down *Bismarck*'s fifth salvo arrived. *Hood* was rent in two by an enormous explosion which appeared at the base of the mainmast aft of the after funnel. The forward part of the ship reared up to the vertical before sinking while the after section remained afloat for some three minutes shrouded in smoke. Of her ship's company of 95 officers and 1,324 men, there were only three

survivors; they were picked up by the destroyer HMS *Electra* after spending nearly two hours in the water.

Cause of the Loss of HMS *Hood*

What exactly caused the explosion that rent HMS *Hood* in two has fascinated historians ever since 24 May 1941. The Admiralty were naturally anxious to ascertain what had happened and convened a Board of Enquiry under the chairmanship of Vice-Admiral Geoffrey Blake. The work of this board proved unsatisfactory, so a second enquiry was set up under Rear Admiral H. T. C. Walker, which concluded that:

> The sinking of the *Hood* was due to a hit from *Bismarck*'s 15″ in or adjacent to *Hood*'s 4″ or 4″ magazines causing them all to explode and wreck the after part of the ship.

The problem in accepting this explanation is that there was no magazine in *Hood* in the area where the explosion was observed: between the mainmast and the after funnel. The nearest magazine was the 4in cordite magazine which lay 65ft aft of the mainmast. A further problem in accepting the Board's explanation is that many observers noted a delay of some seconds between *Bismarck*'s fifth salvo landing alongside *Hood* and the explosion – if a magazine explosion was the cause, then the explosion would have been practically simultaneous with the fall of shot. Thirdly, most observers recalled that the explosion was essentially noiseless – witnesses of magazine explosions in other British ships (HMS *Natal*, *Bulwark* and *Vanguard* in the First World War) all commented on the terrific noise of the explosion.

In an attempt to provide a more valid explanation, the Director of Naval Construction, Sir Stanley Goodall, suggested that the 8in hit from *Prinz Eugen* might have caused one or more of the eight torpedoes (four on each side and each containing a 500lb warhead) for *Hood*'s above-water torpedo tubes to explode. The result would be an explosion where it had actually been observed, which would undoubtedly break the ship's back.

Although attractive, the torpedo theory is probably incorrect. Recent research indicates that the most likely cause of *Hood*'s loss was that a 15in shell from *Bismarck*'s fifth salvo fell alongside *Hood*'s starboard quarter as she began to make the final turn to port. The shell, falling at an angle of between 10.5° and 13.9°, would be capable of penetrating *Hood*'s hull *beneath the armoured belt*, and provided that the fuse was not rendered useless by the impact with the water, the point of detonation would be near the after magazines, which contained over 155 tons of cordite. The detonation of a 15in shell in this area would result in a cordite fire causing a build-up of gas. For a while the gas would be contained by the magazine structure – hence the delay between the arrival of *Bismarck*'s fifth salvo and the explosion – but when pressure became too great it would have taken the line of least resistance and burst forward, blowing out the bulkhead into the engine room before venting up through the exhaust vents located on the upper deck *between the mainmast and the funnel*. Although the venting of the gas into the engine room would have relieved pressure somewhat, it would not be sufficient to prevent the cordite fire from tearing *Hood* apart. To those watching from *Prince of Wales, Suffolk, Norfolk, Bismarck* and *Prinz Eugen*, the explosion would have been visible as spectacular jets of flame around the base of the mainmast.

British Break Off the Action

Prince of Wales was now left to endure the combined fire of *Bismarck* and *Prinz Eugen*. She quickly received one 15in hit on her bridge, causing many casualties. A further three 15in hits were received, which did much superficial damage. To make matters worse, the battleship's new armament was giving trouble – for a period only three-gun salvoes could be fired. With Admiral Holland killed in *Hood*, Admiral Wake-Walker was now the senior officer. He had to decide whether to renew the action with one damaged battleship, or to break off the action but continue to shadow *Bismarck* until Tovey arrived with superior forces. It was a difficult choice to make: Wake-Walker opted for the latter, and although his actions were eventually approved by the Admiralty, there were those who wished to turn him into a scapegoat for what had happened.

Bismarck herself did not emerge from the fight unscathed. She had received three 14in hits from *Prince of Wales*, one of which had penetrated an oil fuel tank and caused the loss of nearly 1,000 tonnes of fuel. Other damage included the flooding of No 4 generator room and the slow leakage of water into No 2 boiler room. Concerned about the damage, Lutjens decided to break off 'Rheinübung' and head for repairs at St Nazaire, while releasing *Prinze Eugen* for independent commerce-raiding operations. Detaching *Prinz Eugen* proved difficult as Lutjens could not shake off *Prince of Wales, Suffolk* and *Norfolk* which were doggedly following him. Eventually, on the evening of 24 May, *Prinz Eugen* successfully got away, leaving *Bismarck* to face the British on her own.

Tovey Acts to Slow *Bismarck* Down

Admiral Tovey was concerned that *Bismarck* might yet escape and he had to slow her down so that his main force, steaming down from the NE, could bring her to action. Accordingly he ordered *Victorious* to proceed ahead, escorted by the 2nd Cruiser Squadron, and launch an air strike. The weather could scarcely have been worse when at 2200 on 24 May nine Swordfish of No 825 Squadron took off, led by Lieutenant-Commander Eugene Esmonde.

The attack was pressed home just after midnight on 24/25 May. Only one torpedo struck *Bismarck*, on the armoured belt on her starboard side, doing no damage. Nevertheless, the violent manoeuvring required to avoid the torpedoes increased water pressure on the hull sections damaged in the *Hood* action, and the hitherto controllable flooding into No 2 boiler room became uncontrollable and speed had to be reduced to 16 knots.

Bismarck Shakes off her Shadowers – Temporarily

Lutjens' staff had been observing the movements of the British cruisers carefully and at 0300 on 25 May succeeced in breaking contact by steaming round in a circle to starboard of *Suffolk*. However, the success of the manoeuvre was negated by Lutjens' careless use of his wireless. At 0727 on 25 May he sent a short signal indicating that the British were still in contact, although by this stage they were not, and at 0900 he broadcast a lengthy 30-minute signal describing the *Hood* action. In doing so Lutjens had given his position away for although the DF position was initially wrongly plotted by the British, the mistake was soon realized.

The Royal Air Force was co-operating with the Navy in providing long-range air reconnaissance patrols from Iceland. The RAF covered the Denmark Strait, Iceland-Faroes gap and also *Bismarck*'s route should she be making for a French port. At 1030 on 26 May, *Bismarck* was sighted heading for the French coast by a Catalina of No 209 Squadron. Contact had been regained.

'Force H' Launch an Air Strike

Steaming up from Gibraltar and making heavy progress in the face of a north-westerly gale were the ships of Vice-Admiral Sir James Somerville's 'Force H'. However, after the disaster which befell *Hood*, Tovey ordered Somerville not to engage *Bismarck* directly with *Renown* – which was a ship of similar characteristics to *Hood*.

On 26 May, while *Ark Royal*'s aircraft prepared to launch the strike, the cruiser *Sheffield* was detached to shadow *Bismarck*. Unfortunately the signal ordering this movement was not repeated to *Ark Royal*, with nearly tragic consequences: the fourteen Swordfish mistook *Sheffield* for *Bismarck* and dropped eleven torpedoes. Five of the torpedoes exploded prematurely and the remainder were neatly avoided by some smart ship-handling by Captain Larcom. 'Sorry for the kipper' was the remorseful signal sent to *Sheffield* by a contrite Swordfish.

By 1720 the Swordfish had all been recovered by *Ark Royal* and were being rearmed for a second sortie. The strike took off at 1910 and consisted of fifteen aircraft – four from No 810 Squadron, four from No 818 Squadron and seven from No 820 Squadron – and was over by 2125. Three hits were scored: two on the armour belt amidships, which did little or no damage, but the third sealed *Bismarck*'s fate. Four aircraft were damaged by flak splinters – one machine later had to be written off – and one officer and a rating were wounded. It was a small price to pay.

The third torpedo jammed *Bismarck*'s twin rudders with 12° of port helm on. The tiller flat soon flooded and had to be evacuated. Flooding spread to adjacent compartments and although damage control teams succeeded in shoring up the bulkheads, the heavy seas which were running prevented collision mats from being placed over the hole in the hull. Desperate attempts were made to steer the ship using a hand rudder, but were doomed to failure. Lindemann tried to con his stricken ship from the bridge using differing combinations of engines and revolutions, all equally unsuccessful. At 2054 Lutjens reported to Group (West) that the ship could not be steered. Morale on *Bismarck* slumped.

British Destroyers Attack

The 4th Destroyer Flotilla, consisting of *Cossack*, *Sikh*, *Maori* and the Polish *Piorun*, all under the command of the formidable Captain Philip Vian, had been part of the escort for convoy WS.8B but had been ordered to reinforce Tovey. Typically Vian disregarded the order and chose to go after *Bismarck* on his own. The flotilla made contact with *Bismarck* just before midnight and throughout the rest of the night made a series of attacks in heavy weather in the dark. Six attacks were carried out between 0121 and 0656 on 27 May, but no hits were scored despite claims to the contrary. Although their attacks produced no material results, they undoubtedly had an effect on *Bismarck*'s young and inexperienced ship's company, who were at action stations for most of the night and who can have had few opportunities for rest.

German Plans to Save *Bismarck*

During the night of 26/27 May Lutjens seems to have realized the hopelessness of his position. At 2140 he sent his famous signal to the Führer vowing to fight to the last shell and appealing for a U-boat to come and take off the ship's war diary. Admiral Dönitz ordered all U-boats to the vicinity – even those without torpedoes – and a patrol line was set up consisting of *U.48*, *U.73*, *U.74*, *U.97*, *U.98* and *U.556* (ironically this last boat, under the command of Lt Wohlfahrt, had been 'adopted' by *Bismarck*) across *Bismarck*'s expected line of advance in the hope that she would draw the British fleet in front of the waiting U-boats.

In the event only *U.556* – which had expended all her torpedoes earlier in her patrol – came in contact with the British ships. She sighted 'Force H' before being put down by a destroyer and was later harried by aircraft. At midnight on 26/27 May Wohlfahrt could see *Bismarck*'s gunfire as she fought off the destroyers, but could do nothing to help her and at 0400 he turned over the task of sending homing signals to *U.74*. At 1000 on 27 May Wohlfahrt received an order to collect *Bismarck*'s war diary, but by then it was too late. The efforts to send U-boats to *Bismarck*'s assistance were a mark of desperation since in the worsening weather it is difficult to see what they could achieve.

Co-operation with the Luftwaffe proved equally unsuccessful. However, given *Bismarck*'s position, the earliest that aircraft flying from France could have given cover would have been 0630.

The Final Action: 27 May 1941

Bismarck now had little way on and often hove to in the rising seas. It was only a matter of time before the ships of the Home Fleet caught up with her. The cruiser *Norfolk* regained contact at 0753 and transmitted *Bismarck*'s position, course and speed to Tovey, who finally sighted *Bismarck* at 0842.

Because of the haze, rangefinding was difficult and *King George V* used her Type 284 gunnery radar to obtain the first range. *Rodney* opened fire at 0847, followed a minute later by *King George V*, the ranges being 23,400 and 24,600 yards respectively. *Bismarck*, after turning to open her 'A' arcs, returned fire at 0850.

Although *Bismarck*'s early shooting was remarkably accurate – one shell missed *Rodney* by a matter of yards – she was quickly disabled by the British shellfire. After a quarter of an hour, *Bismarck* had half her main armament disabled and had lost most of her forward fire control equipment, largely due to 16in shellfire from *Rodney*. At 0902 *Norfolk* reported that the guns of *Bismarck*'s 'Anton' (or 'A') turret were depressed and those of 'Bruno' ('B') cocked up in the air, indicating that both turrets were disabled. Control was switched to the after director at 0910, but only four salvoes could be fired before it was disabled. The two after turrets then went into local control, but by 0931 'C' and 'D' turrets were also out of action. The right gun in 'D' turret had been damaged by a premature explosion and only two more

rounds could be fired from the left gun before the turret officer had to order the gun to cease firing for safety reasons. 'C' turret had to cease fire after a hit on the left gun at 0931. The remainder of the action was merely target practice for the British, who ceased firing at 1014 (*Rodney*) and 1021 (*King George V*).

By then *King George V* had fired 339 rounds of 14in, *Rodney* had fired 375 rounds of 16in – and claimed forty hits – while *Norfolk* and *Dorsetshire* had fired 781 rounds of 8in between them. The effect of even a small percentage of the colossal expenditure of ammunition hitting *Bismarck* is almost too horrific to be imagined. Her upper deck and superstructure were a shambles, with many fires raging and continually swept by splinters. One of the most abiding memories of *Bismarck*'s senior survivor of this stage of the action is the courage and devotion to duty of the ship's medical staff. The sick bay was hit and the surgeons could do little more than lay the wounded out on the shell-swept upper deck, comfort them and administer morphine. None of the surgeons or their medical assistants survived the sinking of the ship.

The End of *Bismarck*

After the pounding she had received, *Bismarck* was a battered, listing wreck with her upper deck reduced to a shambles. However, it appeared that she was stubbornly refusing to sink. Tovey therefore ordered the cruiser *Dorsetshire* to finish her off with torpedoes, which she did at 1025. That was the end: at 1040 *Bismarck* turned over and sank with her colours flying. Only 115 of her ship's company of over 2,000 were rescued. Admiral Lutjens was killed in the last stages of the action, possibly when a 14in shell from *King George V* penetrated the armour of 'B' turret, blowing the back off it, and doing much damage to the bridge structure. Kapitän zur See Ernst Lindemann was last seen walking on the forecastle of his sinking ship, refusing all entreaties to save his life, and saluting as his ship sank beneath him.

The debate continues to rage as to whether *Bismarck* was despatched by *Dorsetshire*'s torpedoes or scuttled by her own crew. The true answer will never be known but in many ways the debate is academic. In the rising seas and in her battered condition *Bismarck* could have lasted no longer than a few hours. However, whether she was sunk or scuttled is immaterial in another sense, for nothing can detract from the bravery of her ship's company of whom Admiral Tovey wrote in his dispatch to the Admiralty: 'The *Bismarck* put up a most gallant fight against impossible odds, worthy of the old days of the Imperial German Navy, and she went down with her flag flying.'

1. *Hood* at an early stage of construction at John Brown's Clydebank shipyard in early 1918. The view is from the midships section looking forward along the port side. Visible behind the staging is the outline of the anti-torpedo bulge – an important part of the ship's protection. The bulge consisted of an outer air space, an inner buoyancy space and a 1½in protective bulkhead. The buoyancy space was filled with crushing tubes – sealed steel tubes intended both to absorb the force of an underwater explosion and distribute its force as widely over the protective bulkhead as possible. Behind this bulge was a watertight compartment backed by a compartment containing crush tubes surrounded by oil fuel tanks. This scheme of protection offered considerable immunity from torpedo attack. [*IWM Q.19447*]

2. View looking forward along *Hood*'s upper deck showing the barbettes for 'X' and 'Y' turrets. There is substantial work to be done before the ship is ready for launching as the bow section is still at the frame stage. [*IWM Q.19450*]

3. *Hood* on the slip and ready for launching in August 1918. Three of her four propellers are visible but the armour belt along the port side has yet to be installed. In line with the current naval practice, the installation of the armour belt would be done during the fitting-out period. [*IWM. FL.769*]

4. *Hood* goes down the ways on 22 August 1918, having been launched by Lady Hood, widow of Rear Admiral Horace Hood who was killed in HMS *Invincible* during the Battle of Jutland. *Hood* was the only one of her class to be completed: the other three ships, which had been allocated the names *Rodney*, *Anson* and *Howe*, were all cancelled on 3 March 1917 when it became known that the Germans were not pro-ceeding with the construction of the '*Mackensen*'-class battlecruisers. [*IWM FL. 770*]

5. A fine view of *Hood* lying at anchor in the Firth of Forth on completion in late 1920. The machinery trials were very satisfactory and after gunnery and torpedo firings were concluded, she was commissioned into the Royal Navy on 15 May 1920. One of the most striking aspects of *Hood*'s appearance was the great length of the hull – 810ft overall. Because of the large amount of hull volume taken up by the machinery spaces, the main 15in turrets had to be grouped relatively close together at the ends of the ship. Another feature to note is the flare to the bows, an unusual practice in British capital ship design. The flare was intended to improve seaworthiness but also had the practical purpose of preventing an incoming shell from striking at an angle of 90°, in effect increasing the armour's resistance to penetration. [*Author's Collection*]

6. *Hood* at speed during her trials on completion in March 1920. During the measured mile full-power trial the ship achieved a speed of 32.07 knots with 151,280shp (5 per cent above her designed maximum power). In a subsequent three-hour full-power trial she achieved a speed of 31.8 knots with 150,473shp. However, the trials showed that *Hood* would always be a 'wet' ship, particularly aft where her quarter-deck was often awash. This was due to extra weight put into the ship during construction coupled with her great length, which meant that she cut through the waves rather than ride over them. This was a situation which would worsen throughout *Hood*'s life as her displacement steadily increased. [*IWM Q.17879*]

7. *Hood*'s main armament consisted of eight 15in BL Mk II guns in four twin mountings: 'A' and 'B' turrets (the two forward ones) are shown here. The ship was originally to have been fitted with four Mk I mountings, the type fitted to all British capital ships since the '*Queen Elizabeth*' class. However, lessons learned at the Battle of Jutland (31 May 1916) meant that the Mk I mounting had to be redesigned to meet the demands for action at longer ranges and better safety. The Mk II mounting, which was made by Vickers and only ever fitted in *Hood*, incorporated the following improvements: elevation increased from 20° to 30°, 30ft rangefinders replaced the 15ft instruments on the turret roof, improved anti-flash measures, sighting hoods on turret roof replaced by sighting ports in the turret face, and the hydraulic run-out system replaced by a pneumatic system. [*Author's Collection*]

8. Gun drill on one of *Hood*'s 5.5in 50-cal Mk I guns in January 1924. The gun has just been loaded and the loading numbers of the crew stand behind the breech with the next shell and cordite charge. *Hood* carried twelve of these guns in CP11 mountings – six on each side of the ship. Two on the shelter deck forward were removed in the 1938–9 refit and the remainder went in 1940 to be replaced by three 4in HA/LA Mk XIX mountings. [*Author's Collection*]

9. *Hood* enters Auckland, New Zealand, on 10 May 1924 during the cruise of the 'Special Service Squadron', or 'World Cruise'. In company with *Repulse* and the cruisers *Delhi, Danae, Dragon, Dauntless* and *Dunedin, Hood* circumnavigated the world, calling at Singapore, Australia, New Zealand, and Canada in order to strengthen links in the Commonwealth. *Hood* left Devonport on 27 November 1923 and

returned on 9 September 1924. In the interval she steamed 38,153 miles, crossed the Equator six times, received 752,049 visitors and entertained 37,770 for dinner or other functions. It was a journey never to be repeated by a modern British naval force. [*Author's Collection*]

10. *Hood* passes through the Miraflores Locks in the Panama Canal on 23 July 1924 on the homeward journey during the 'World Cruise'. There was some doubt as to whether she would be able to pass through the locks since the width of the chambers was only 110ft, which gave a clearance of only 30in on either side. To help the huge ship slip through, her sides were smeared with pounds of soft soap. Canal tolls for her passage at 50 cents per ton amounted to $22,399.50c. [*Author's Collection*]

11. *Hood*'s wardroom – a large well furnished compartment but hardly luxurious. The arched opening at the after end of the compartment led through into the anteroom. This and the following internal views of *Hood* were taken in July 1932. [*Wright & Logan*]

12. In contrast this photograph shows Nos 18, 20, 22, 24 and 26 messdeck tables on the port side of the upper deck amidships. There was no natural light since these messdecks lay behind the armoured belt which could not be pierced. *Hood* was one of the first ships in the Royal Navy to adopt the 'General Messing' system for feeding the crew, whereby all food was purchased and cooked centrally rather than by the individual messes. The system was supposed to save the Navy money but was deeply unpopular on the lower deck. Despite their pristine appearance in this photograph, Captain A. F. Pridham, who took over command of *Hood* in 1935, found the messdecks to be infested with vermin; the ship's medical officers had complained for years about inadequate ventilation leading to sporadic outbreaks of TB. [*Wright & Logan*]

13. *Hood*'s 'A' and 'B' turrets present an imposing site trained on the starboard beam. This is a posed photograph as the ship is obviously at anchor (the starboard boom is out) and the 15in armoured director on top of the conning tower with its 30ft rangefinder is still trained fore and aft. [*Wright & Logan*]

14. An equally posed photograph taken on the control platform of the forward engine room – careful examination of the picture reveals that the pressure gauges are set at zero! The two Brown Curtis turbines in the forward engine room drove the wing shafts. Each turbine consisted of an HP and one LP unit driving the shaft through a single reduction gear. The two turbines in the forward engine room also had a cruising turbine (for economy at low power), clutched to the forward end of the HP turbine. [*Wright & Logan*]

15. The control platform of the forward engine room looking from port to starboard and showing the main steam and manoeuvring valve control wheels. *Hood*'s machinery represented a triumph of naval engineering and could develop 144,000shp – the highest of any warship of the time. [*Wright & Logan*]

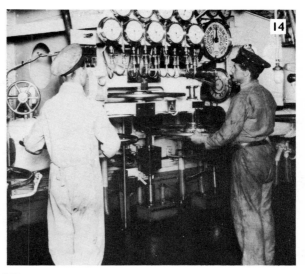

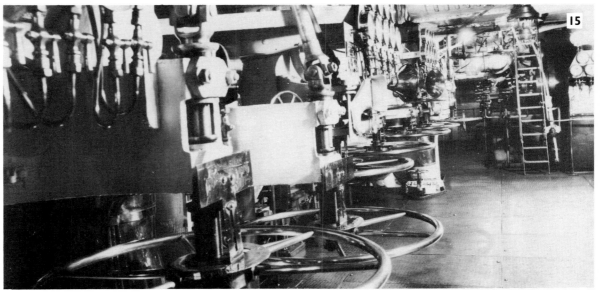

16

17

16. *Hood* leaving Portsmouth in June 1931 on completion of a refit. The photograph shows the ship's aircraft arrangements to good advantage. The catapult, a Folding Mk IV Heavy (FIVH) operated by a series of telescopic rams actuated by compressed air, was fitted on the quarter-deck together with crane for handling the Fairey IIIF seaplane. Two aircraft were allocated to *Hood* although only one could be carried onboard. When not in use the forward half of the catapult folded back against the main section. The arrangement was not a success: the catapult, with the IIIF perched on top of it, proved very vulnerable to weather damage and blast from 'X' and 'Y' turrets and was removed after only ten months' service. [*Wright & Logan*]

17. *Hood* at anchor in July 1934 on completion of a refit at Portsmouth. The most obvious changes visible in this photograph are the paravane derrick rigged against 'A' turret and the pom-pom directors fitted at the after end of the foremast starfish. Note also the port boom swung out with the picket boat secured beneath it. [*Author's Collection*]

18. With her ship's company fallen in, *Hood* leaves Portsmouth in October 1936 bound for the Mediterranean as flagship of the Battle-cruiser Squadron. She was to fly the flag of Admiral Sir Geoffrey Blake – who would later chair the first enquiry into her loss. The photograph clearly shows the flare to Hood's bows and the sweep of the hull from the forecastle down to the after superstructure. [*Wright & Logan*]

19, 20. Two superb views of *Hood* in the Mediterranean in 1937. From 1936 to 1939 *Hood* served as flagship of the Battlecruiser Squadron in the Mediterranean, where she epitomized the power of the Royal Navy in an area which became the focus of international tension during the Spanish Civil War. *Hood*'s main task was to ensure the free passage of merchant shipping against the blockade of Spanish Republican ports imposed by the Nationalist forces. Usually her mere presence was enough to deter the Nationalists, although on 23 April 1937 *Hood* had to reinforce the point by training her 15in guns on the cruiser *Almirante Cervera* which was trying to prevent three British merchant ships entering Bilbao. Note the red-white-blue identification stripes painted on 'B' turret. [*Author's Collection*]

21. A magnificent view of *Hood* at anchor at Spithead on 17 May 1937 for the Coronation Naval Review. At public occasions such as fleet reviews, *Hood* represented the power and might of the Royal Navy to the world. The ship seemed to possess a unique aura of invincibility. But the fact remains that *Hood* went through her career without a single major refit and by the end of the 1930s was desperately in need of modification. That the work was not done earlier was due to financial constraints in the inter-war period and because *Hood* was a relatively new ship. [*IWM DS.595/14*]

22. A bearded Petty Officer points to splinter damamge suffered by *Hood* on 26 September 1939 when she was bombed by German aircraft – her first taste of combat. *Hood* was at Portsmouth having just completed a refit when war broke out and was ordered to join the Home Fleet as Flagship of the Battlecruiser Squadron. She was ordered to sea with *Repulse* to provide heavy cover for cruisers and destroyers which were escorting the damaged submarine *Spearfish* home. The attack was delivered by Junkers Ju 88s of KG 30 but only one bomb hit the ship, a glancing blow on the quarter. No serious damage was done but the ship's side was liberally peppered with splinters. [*IWM A.172*]

23. A group of *Hood*'s ship's company, with mascot, in good spirits on the forecastle in May 1940 after the ship had completed another refit at Devonport and before she sailed for the Mediterranean to join 'Force H' under the command of Vice-Admiral Sir James Somerville. The most significant work done in this refit was the removal of all the 5.5in guns and their associated control equipment and magazine arrangements. Alterations visible in the photograph include the UP (Unrotated Projectile) mounting on 'B' turret – one of five such mountings fitted – and the removal of the 15ft rangefinder from the aloft director tower. [*IWM A.176*]

24. *Hood*'s 'X' and 'Y' turrets in action during the bombardment of the French Fleet at Oran on 3 July 1940. Following the armistice concluded with the Germans by France's Pétain government, the British Government was resolutely opposed to the idea of the French fleet falling into German hands. 'Force H', consisting of *Hood, Valiant, Resolution*, the aircraft-carrier *Ark Royal*, cruisers *Arethusa* and *Enterprise*, and eleven destroyers, was despatched to Oran to offer the French authorities three alternatives: join the British; sail to a British or French West Indies port for internment; or scuttle their ships. The French rejected the offer and shortly after 6pm on 3 July Somerville's ships opened fire. After a brief action one French battleship, *Bretagne*, had blown up and two others had been beached, badly damaged. It was a melancholy event which continues to arouse the deepest antagonism in France. [*IWM HU.51562*]

25. After the action at Oran, *Hood* remained in the Mediterranean with 'Force H'. On 9 July 1940 Somerville was ordered to cover a strike by *Ark Royal*'s aircraft on the Italian airfield at Cagliari. During the run-in, 'Force H' was subjected to heavy Italian air attack with sticks of bombs falling close around *Hood*, as shown in the photograph, and *Ark Royal*. Somerville decided that the operation was unsound and ordered a recall to Gibraltar. This would be *Hood*'s last appearance in the Mediterranean; in August 1940 she returned to Britain to become Flagship of the Battlecruiser Squadron, Home Fleet. [*IWM ZZZ.8056c*]

26. Twenty years after *Hood* was launched on the Clyde, another capital ship, battleship 'F', later named *Bismarck*, was taking shape on Slip 9 of Blohm und Voss's Hamburg shipyard. *Bismarck* was the most powerful capital ship built in Germany since the First World War. The photograph, taken on 10 September 1938, shows her complete up to the level of the upper deck. The barbettes are visible for, from bottom to top, 'Anton', 'Bruno', 'Caesar' and 'Dora' 38cm turrets (the Kriegsmarine coded their ships' after turrets 'C' and 'D' rather than the 'X' and 'Y' used by the Royal Navy), together with the 15cm mountings down each side of the ship. [*Foto Druppel RM.4576*]

27. *Bismarck* being launched on 14 February 1939. The ceremony was performed by Frau Dorothea von Loewenfeld, grand-daughter of Prince Otto von Bismarck. As the ship began her glide down the ways into the Elbe, a sign was revealed on the bows showing her name and the family crest on the bow was uncovered. The photograph shows *Bismarck* with a straight stem which would in time be replaced by the graceful, raked 'Atlantic' bow. [*IWM HU.39770, Hoffmann Collection*]

28. *Bismarck* alongside the fitting-out jetty at Hamburg, showing a portion of the armour belt (of between 10½ and 12½in thickness) being swung into position. Her pro-tection differed little from that of the *'Baden'* class, the Imperial German Navy's last dreadnoughts, but greater emphasis was placed on horizontal rather than vertical protection. The scaffolding around the bow is most likely associated with the building of the 'Atlantic' bow. [*Bundesarchiv B29/4/16A*]

29. Another view of *Bismarck*'s side showing part of the armour belt already in place. The dark parts of the hull are the sections of the armour belt already in position. Note the bolt holes in the side of the hull for securing the belt to the ship's side. [*Bundesarchiv*]

30. *Bismarck* in the giant floating dock at Blohm und Voss's Hamburg yard while work was carried out on her underwater hull fittings. The photograph shows the full flare of the 'Atlantic' bow, together with the remains of the launching cradle still welded on to the hull either side of the stem; the latter was designed to take the weight of the hull during the critical moment in the launching process when the stern was afloat but the bow still on the slip. The white circle at the bottom of the stem is the Bugschutzgerät (bow protection gear) to which the paravanes, streamed by the ship when proceeding through waters likely to be mined, would be secured. [*Bundesarchiv B29/3/37*]

31. Elements of *Bismarck*'s armament on the jetty and ready for installation. From left to right: a 15cm mounting; the lower sections of a 38cm mounting, the white structure at the top being the upper ends of the shell hoists; and a turret base for a 38cm mounting. Behind the turret base is the breech end of a 38cm gun wrapped in tarpaulin. [*Bundesarchiv B34/5/21*]

32. The installation of 'Caesar' 38cm mounting. The gunhouse floor with the trunnions already erected is being lowered on to the roller path. The ball bearings supporting the turret and the gearing with which the electric training motor engaged are all visible in the photograph. Beneath the gunhouse lay the magazines with the shell rooms beneath them. The turret was served by hydraulic hoists which ran direct to the gunhouse. As was often the case in German naval mountings of the Second World War period, safety precautions were sketchy by British standards. To the right of the photograph is the covered barbette for 'Dora' turret. [*Bundesarchiv B33/7/2*]

33. One of *Bismarck*'s twelve Wagner boilers being lowered into position for installation deep in the hull. The main machinery developed 138,000shp, sufficient for a top speed of 29 knots. However her endurance, 8,410nm at 15 knots, was less than that of her predecessors *Scharnhorst* and *Gneisenau*, and did not make *Bismarck* the ideal ship for commerce raiding in the Atlantic. [*Bundesarchiv B34/3/369*]

34. *Bismarck*'s main armament consisted of eight 38cm SKC/34 guns of the type shown firing in the photograph of her sister ship *Tirpitz*. The gun weight, including breech mechanism, was 109.2 tons and it fired a 1,764lb shell to a range of 38,280 yards with the gun at 29.1° elevation. [*IWM Tirpitz Collection*]

35. *Bismarck* manoeuvring away from the fitting-out jetty at Hamburg on 15 September 1940. That evening she anchored in Brunsbüttel Roads in order to make the passage through the Kiel Canal into the Baltic the next day. At Kiel the ship underwent a series of preliminary trials before proceeding to Gotenhafen (Gdynia) on the Baltic coast for a proper work-up. [*IWM HU.3279*]

36. View looking forward over the roof of *Bismarck*'s armoured conning tower, with the very cramped navigating bridge in front, on to 'Anton' and 'Bruno' turrets. On the roof of the conning tower, protected by 350mm-thick armour, three gunnery director periscopes are visible, together with a number of navigational periscopes. Further down on the port side of 'Anton' turret, a party of seamen is being mustered for duty by a petty officer. [*Bundesarchiv*]

37. View looking aft down *Bismarck*'s starboard side taken from just forward of the barbette for 'Bruno' turret. By the side of the bridge superstructure a party of seamen is mustering for what appears to be some sort of kit inspection, while behind them are the S.1 and S.2 twin 15cm mountings. Note the paravane stowed aft of the barbette for 'Bruno' turret and the extended hinged bridge wings — necessary in a ship of such wide beam when navigating through confined spaces such as the Kiel Canal. [*Bundesarchiv*]

38. View looking aft down the port side from the catapult deck showing the hangar door. *Bismarck* was equipped to take six Arado Ar 196 seaplanes for reconnaissance purposes. Abreast the funnel were two single hangars, while under the mainmast and boat stowage was a larger hangar which held two aircraft. If all six aircraft were embarked, two would have to be kept on the catapults since only four could be stowed in the hangars. [*Bundesarchiv*]

39

40

41

39. *Bismarck* shows off her fine, modern lines during her trials in Kiel Bay in late 1940. The censor has altered her appearance somewhat by removing the mattress radar aerial from the rangefinder on the foretop. *Bismarck* was commissioned into the Kriegsmarine on 24 August 1940 under the command of Kapitän zur See Ernst Lindemann. She then underwent an exhaustive series of trials and exercises in the Baltic to prepare the ship and crew for operations. She returned to Blohm und Voss between December 1940 and March 1941 for the finishing touches to be applied by the builders before returning to Gotenhafen for further exercises.

40. The heavy cruiser *Prinz Eugen* armed with eight 20cm guns, *Bismarck*'s partner in 'Rheinübung'; the similarity in appearance between the two ships was intentional. The role of the two ships were complementary in 'Rheinübung': *Bismarck* would take care of any capital ship escort which had frustrated *Scharnhorst* and *Gneisenau*'s activities in the earlier Operation 'Berlin', while *Prinz Eugen* rolled up the merchant shipping.

41. The two ships exercised extensively together in the Baltic throughout April and May 1941. This photograph taken from onboard *Prinz Eugen* shows the cruiser fuelling *Bismarck* by the astern method, favoured in the Kriegsmarine as opposed to the abreast method. *Bismarck*'s immense beam, which made her such a stable gun platform even in the heaviest seas, is clearly visible. [*IWM HU.376*]

42. Admiral Gunther Lutjens, commander of the *Bismarck/Prinz Eugen* task force. Lutjens entered the Imperial German Navy in 1907 and spent the Great War in destroyers. In February and March 1941 he commanded the battlecruisers *Scharnhorst* and *Gneisenau* during Operation 'Berlin', a commerce raiding voyage in the Atlantic, so he was the ideal choice to command Operation 'Rheinübung'. Lutjens had a dry, serious disposition which could be seen as forbidding but which concealed a highly intelligent, able and courageous character. However, he was a commander not given to confiding his intentions to his subordinates and would shoulder the entire burden of command himself. [*IWM A.14897*]

43. Hitler stands on the bridge of the tender *Hela* as he approaches *Bismarck* for his only visit to the ship at Gotenhafen on 1 May 1941. He toured the ship, expressing great interest in the fire control instruments, then had lunch with Lutjens and his staff, during which the forthcoming operation was discussed. Those present recorded that Hitler displayed little interest in or enthusiasm for naval operations. Note the after main armament director trained to starboard, showing off the mattress aerial for the FuMo.213 radar set. [*IWM*]

44. *Bismarck* under way in the early stage of 'Rheinübung'. *Bismarck* and *Prinz Eugen* left Gotenhafen early on the morning of 19 May and proceeded through the Belts, Kattegat and into the Skagerrak on 20 May.

Her passage did not go unreported: the Swedish cruiser *Gotland* sighted the battleship and reported her presence to Stockholm, where pro-British officers passed the news to the British Naval Attache. The Admiralty knew that *Bismarck* was on her way to sea by early the next morning. This photograph was taken from *Prinz Eugen* and shows *Bismarck* still wearing her dazzle camouflage. [*IWM HU.374, Schmaelenbach Collection*]

45. *Bismarck* at anchor in Grimstadtfjord, Norway, on 21 May. While on their way into Grimstadtfjord the German ships were spotted by members of the Norwegian resistance who radioed a sighting report to London, which was seen as confirmation of the report from Sweden. *Prinz Eugen* and the three destroyers of the escort screen went further up the fjord to fuel but, surprisingly in view of her limited endurance, *Bismarck* did not. While she was at anchor her distinctive black and white dazzle stripes were over-painted by standard dark grey. [*IWM HU.375, Schmaelenbach Collection*]

46. It was while the German ships were at Grimstadtfjord that definite proof of their sortie was obtained by the British. On receipt of the warning from the British Naval Attache in Sweden, an air reconnaissance of the Norwegian coast was organized and Flying Officer Michael Suckling took this famous photograph at 1315 on 21 May. A strike by Hudson and Whitley aircraft was ordered but because of poor weather only two Hudsons bombed the area. It was a futile mission for *Bismarck* and *Prinz Eugen* had sailed at 1930, although this news was not confirmed by air reconnaissance until the evening of 22 May. 'Rheinübung' was under way. [*IWM CS.159*]

47

49

48

50

47. Admiral Sir John Tovey, Commander-in-Chief of the Home Fleet. On receipt of the news that *Bismarck* had sailed, Tovey had to make his dispositions. His fear was that *Bismarck* would break out undetected into the Atlantic and ravage the convoys. At this point it was most important to warn the cruiser patrols of *Bismarck*'s approach; the cruisers were not to attack her but to shadow her until superior forces could be brought to bear. The cruisers *Suffolk* and *Norfolk* patrolling the Denmark Strait were warned that *Bismarck* might use that route into the Atlantic, rather than the Iceland-Faroes route which was patrolled by *Arethusa*, *Manchester* and *Birmingham*. Tovey sailed from Scapa Flow on 22 May with the battleship *King George V*, the aircraft-carrier *Victorious*, four cruisers and seven destroyers, being joined by the battlecruiser *Repulse* on the 23rd.

48. Vice-Admiral Sir James Somerville (right) on the flight deck of HMS *Ark Royal* with the carrier's commanding officer, Captain L. Maund. Somerville was commanding 'Force H' which consisted of *Ark Royal*, the battlecruiser *Renown* and the cruiser *Sheffield*. One of the Admiralty's main priorities was to protect convoys at sea and at the time there were no fewer than eleven in the Atlantic. One of the biggest was the troop convoy WS.8B and on 24 May 'Force H' was ordered to sea

to protect it. Somerville's ships were then at Gibraltar but were under way within an hour of the signal being received. [*IWM A.5825*]

49. HMS *Suffolk* on patrol in the Denmark Strait in 1941. With her sister ship *Norfolk*, she formed the 1st Cruiser Squadron under the command of Rear Admiral W. F. Wake-Walker. When news that *Bismarck* was out was received, *Suffolk* was fuelling at Hvalfjord in Iceland but she hurriedly put to sea to join her sister ship. At 1922 on 23 May *Suffolk* sighted *Bismarck* and *Prinz Eugen* heading south through the Denmark Strait. Despite being fired on by *Bismarck* – *Norfolk* received five 38cm salvoes which straddled her – the two cruisers settled down to shadow using their radar, and report the Germans' movements to Admiral Holland in *Hood*, coming up from

the SE, and Admiral Tovey. [*IWM A.4168*]

50. Able Seaman Alfred Newall, one of *Suffolk*'s lookouts, was the first to sight *Bismarck* as she loomed out of the mist on 23 May. Although it was smart work by a lookout which had won the first sighting of *Bismarck*, it was the cruisers' radar, *Suffolk* with the new Type 284 and *Norfolk* with the older Type 268P, which enabled them to stay in touch. The German B-Dienst (signals intelligence experts) teams in *Bismarck* were soon aware that their movements were being accurately reported by the shadowing cruisers. The discovery that the British possessed radar as good if not better than their own was to prove highly unsettling to the Germans. [*IWM A.4216*]

51. *Hood* at Hvalfjord, Iceland, in April 1941. Tovey was not content with warning his cruisers. He guessed that Lutjens would head for the Denmark Strait so on 22 May ordered *Hood*, in company with *Prince of Wales* and six destroyers under the command of Vice-Admiral Lancelot Holland, to proceed to Iceland to be in a favourable position to intercept the German ships as they broke out into the Atlantic. As the ships sped north the sighting reports from *Suffolk* and *Norfolk* were received and Holland altered course for the Denmark Strait. It was evident to Holland that action would be joined early on the morning of 24 May. One of the crew of *Electra*, one of the six escorting destroyers, remembered watching the big battlecruiser cleaving through the waves, her ensign taut in the wind, and thought her absolutely unsinkable.

52. The battleship *Prince of Wales* commanded by Captain J. C. Leach, second of the '*King George V*' class and *Hood*'s consort on her last voyage. Armed with ten 14in guns and equipped with the latest in radar fire control, *Prince of Wales* was a formidable adversary – on paper. The ship had been commissioned on 31 March 1941 and had only just completed her work-up. Moreover, technicians from Vickers-Armstrongs were still on board, making last-minute adjustments to the loading machinery of the ship's main armament. [*IWM A.3869*]

53. The classic photograph of *Bismarck* in action, taken from *Prinz Eugen*. 'C' and 'D' turrets have just fired on a bearing of 310° and their flash throws *Bismarck*'s superstructure into relief. The action began early in the morning of 24 May as Holland's ships encountered the two German vessels, *Prinz Eugen* leading *Bismarck*, steering south-west. *Hood* opened fire at 0552 at a range of 25,000 yards, followed shortly afterwards by *Bismarck*.

54. The midships section of *Hood* photographed in 1940 while the ship's company 'paint ship'. The German gunnery was extraordinarily accurate, with the third salvo hitting the ship amidships at the base of the mainmast – although this hit may have been caused by an 8in shell from *Prinz Eugen*. This hit caused a fire among the ready-use ammunition for the 4in mountings and URP (Unrotated Projectile) mountings visible in the photograph. The fire burnt with a vivid pink glow which was clearly discernible in both German ships. *Bismarck*'s fourth salvo fell short, but the fifth would be the fatal one. [*IWM A.180*]

55 <!-- label on image -->

55. The last known photograph of *Hood*, taken from *Prince of Wales*. *Hood* bears 341° from *Prince of Wales* at a range of 1,070 yards. The gun barrels are those of 'A' turret, trained on the port quarter. Moments later *Hood* would begin a turn to port which would open her 'A' arcs and allow all four turrets to be brought into action. The '2 Blue' signal ordering such a turn was flying but had not been hauled down when *Bismarck*'s fifth salvo arrived, and *Hood* was rent in two by a huge explosion between the after funnel and the base of the mainmast. The stern portion of the ship sank quickly while the bow portion rose up to the vertical before sliding back into the sea.

56. The view from *Prinz Eugen* shortly after *Hood* had blown up. From left to right the various shell splashes and smoke are identified as follows: 14in shell splashes from *Prince of Wales* falling hundreds of yards short; smoke from *Norfolk*; 15in shell splashes from *Bismarck*; smoke from the explosion of *Hood*; smoke from *Prince of Wales* as she disengages. [*IWM HU.384, Schmalenbach Collection*]

57. The foremost Mk V above-water torpedo tube on *Hood*'s starboard side. What caused the sudden overwhelming explosion which rent the battlecruiser in two will never be known, but there have been numerous theories; one is that a shell

56 <!-- label on image -->

from *Bismarck*'s fifth salvo exploded near the above-water tubes, causing a sympathetic explosion of the torpedoes. Such an explosion in an area already weakened by fire and earlier damage, it is argued, could have caused the ship to break in half. The theory was considered and discounted by the Board of Enquiry.

58. There were three survivors from *Hood*'s ships company of 1,419. All three were rescued by the destroyer *Electra*, shown in her pre-war state. Midshipman William Dundas and Signalman Ted Briggs both got out of *Hood*'s bridge, Dundas by kicking through a window on the starboard side and Briggs by leaving through the door on the port side.

59

60

59. Able Seaman Bob Tilburn, the third survivor, with his little brother while on survivor's leave in the UK. Tilburn was stationed at one of the 4in mountings on the port side of the ship and was ordered to take cover after the ready-use ammunition on the boat deck caught fire. Seeing one of his 'oppos' killed and another disembowelled, Tilburn rushed to the rail to be sick. As he did so, *Hood* began her final list to port and Tilburn was washed over the side. His last view of the ship was of her bows towering above him.

60. Vice-Admiral Geoffrey Blake who chaired the first, and unsatisfactory enquiry, into the loss of *Hood*. On 28 May the First Sea Lord, Admiral Sir Dudley Pound, ordered an enquiry into the cause of her loss and Blake submitted his report on 2 June – only nine days after *Hood* went down. The report consisted of two typewritten pages of conclusions with no supporting evidence. Unbelievably, Blake had not thought it necessary to take evidence from Briggs and Tilburn, the two non-commissioned survivors. The VCNS commented that 'the report . . . does not give me confidence that a searching enquiry has been carried out'. [*IWM A.17048*]

61. Accordingly a second enquiry was ordered, under the chairmanship of Rear Admiral H. T. C. Walker (seen in 1945 by which time he had been promoted Vice-Admiral). Walker began his work in August 1941 and presented his report on 12 September having heard evidence from 176 witnesses of the explosion, including all three of *Hood*'s survivors. Walker's findings were that a 15in shell from *Bismarck*'s fifth salvo caused the after 15in and 4in magazines to explode, wrecking the after part of the ship. Recent research suggests that it was uncontrolled burning of cordite charges, as a result of one of *Bismarck*'s 15in shells penetrating *Hood*'s hull beneath the armour belt, rather than a magazine explosion which was responsible for her loss. [*IWM A.30995*]

62

63

62. *Bismarck*, having moved to the starboard side of *Prinz Eugen*, opens fire on *Prince of Wales* with 'C' and 'D' turrets. By this stage the range had come down to 14,000 yards and Captain Lindemann wanted to continue the action and pursue *Prince of Wales* and destroy her. He was overruled by Lutjens who did not want to be distracted from his principal mission against British trade. According to many accounts the disagreement between the two men was a serious one and morale fell among the crew since they could not understand why *Prince of Wales* was being allowed to escape. [*IWM HU.380, Schmalenbach Collection*]

63. Damage to *Prince of Wales* sustained in the action with *Bismarck*. After the loss of *Hood*, *Prince of Wales* endured the fire of both German ships before retiring under smoke. One 38cm shell passed through her bridge without exploding but killing all there except for Captain Leach and the Chief Yeoman of Signals. This view, looking across towards the after funnel from the starboard side of the ship, shows splinter and blast damage to the funnel casing and surrounding area from the partial burst of a 15in shell which exploded about 9ft 6in above the boat deck.

64. View from the port aircraft crane of *Prince of Wales* looking aft and inboard showing splinter holes in the deck caused by the same 15in shell as in the preceding photograph. *Prince of Wales* was hit seven times in all by *Bismarck* and *Prinz Eugen* but did not sustain serious damage. It was mechanical breakdowns and errors in drill with the main armament which caused Captain Leach, reluctantly, to break off the action.

65. *Bismarck* did not get away from the action unscathed. After *Hood* had blown up, *Prince of Wales* switched on her Type 281 radar and succeeded in determining *Bismarck*'s range with some success. This well-known photograph, taken from *Prinz Eugen* during a change of station on 24 May 1941, shows *Bismarck* after the action and is the last picture of her taken from the German side. She had been struck by three 14in shells from *Prince of*

Wales: one penetrated an oil fuel tank, causing massive fuel spillage and the bow-down angle evident in the photograph; the second caused only minor damage; while the third struck her side armour amidships, causing a leak and reducing her maximum speed by 2 knots. As a result of this damage, Admiral Lutjens resolved to abandon 'Rhein-übung' and head for a French port on the Atlantic coast for repairs.

66. Swordfish torpedo-bombers ranged at the after end of the flight deck of HMS *Victorious*. Although *Bismarck* was damaged, there was still the possibility that she would escape unless her speed could be reduced by torpedo attack. Accordingly Tovey detached the new aircraft-carrier *Victorious* to proceed and launch a strike using the nine Swordfish of No 826 Squadron led by Lieutenant-Commander Eugene Esmonde. The attack was pressed home in atrocious weather on the evening of 24 May and scored one hit on the starboard side on the main armoured belt, but without doing any damage. However, the high-speed manoeuvring required to avoid the torpedoes had increased pressure on the sections of *Bismarck*'s hull damaged during the *Hood* action. The bulkhead between No 4 generator room and No 2 port boiler room ruptured and the boiler room had to be shut down. The collision mat over the hit in the bows parted and speed had to be reduced while the damage was made good. [*IWM A.4090*]

67. Flying Officer Dennis Briggs, the pilot of Catalina 'Z' of No 209 Squadron, RAF, who sighted *Bismarck* on 26 May. Following the strike by *Victorious*'s aircraft, *Bismarck* succeeded in shaking off the shadowing *Norfolk* and *Suffolk*. But having given the cruisers the slip, Lutjens then transmitted a very long, 30-minute message on the morning of 25 May which was picked up by British DF. However, Lutjens' luck held for the DF position was plotted incorrectly and the mistake not realized until the evening of 25 May. Meanwhile the RAF flew long-range reconnaissances and it was Briggs's Catalina which finally found *Bismarck*. He remained in contact for 15 minutes despite being taken under heavy fire, but the sighting was all that Tovey needed to know. [*IWM CH.2763*]

68. A Swordfish returns to *Ark Royal* after her strike on 26 May. Tovey with *King George V* and *Rodney* was 130 miles away from *Bismarck* but still needed to slow her down, so he ordered a torpedo attack by Swordfish from *Ark Royal*. The strike was launched at 1450 with fourteen Swordfish and nearly ended in tragedy for the aircraft had not been told that the cruiser *Sheffield* was operating independently and they attacked her, mistaking her for *Bismarck*. Masterly manoeuvring by Captain Larcom saved his ship and the Swordfish returned to *Ark Royal* to rearm. The second strike was launched at 1910 and succeeded in inflicting a crippling blow on *Bismarck*. [*IWM A.4100*]

69

70

69. The erratic wake left by *Bismarck* after *Ark Royal*'s second attack on 26 May. The puny 18in torpedoes could do little against the German battleship's massively protected sides but one of them detonated under her starboard quarter, wrecking the steering mechanism and jamming the rudders at an angle of 12° to port. The battleship began to turn in a wide circle to port and to steer to the north-west away from St Nazaire, into the wind and towards the enemy. This torpedo hit sealed *Bismarck*'s fate.

70, 71. However, *Sheffield*'s troubles were not over. She continued to shadow *Bismarck* until 2137 when the battleship was sighted coming out of the fog towards her. *Bismarck* fired six salvoes of 15in, the first of which consisted of HE shell which had been loaded for use against *Ark Royal*'s aircraft. These shells burst on hitting the water and splinters scythed across *Sheffield*'s decks, killing three men and wounding many more. The photographs show the crew of the after director control tower pointing to splinter damage while Paymaster Lieutenant G. B. Harris inspects splinter damage in the wardroom; the portraits of HM The King and Queen were dislodged but not damaged. [*IWM A.4092 and A.4095*]

71

72. Captain Philip Vian, commanding officer of the destroyer *Cossack*. In company with *Zulu, Maori* and the Polish *Piorun*, Vian took over the task of shadowing *Bismarck* during the night of 26/27 May. Vian soon realized that *Bismarck*'s speed was so reduced that interception by the Home Fleet on 27 May was inevitable, provided that contact could be maintained. He therefore ordered his ships to shadow rather than attack, but from 2121 until 0656 on 27 May the three British destroyers (*Piorun* did not attack since she was not familiar with Vian's procedures) launched six attacks but scored no hits. However, the strain of repelling these continual attacks throughout the night must have had an effect on *Bismarck*'s crew who can have had little opportunity for rest. [*IWM A.1595*]

73. *Rodney* engages *Bismarck* in the final stages of the action. By the morning of 27 May *Bismarck* could not steer and had little way on. A torpedo strike by *Ark Royal*'s Swordfish was called off because of poor visibility and the field was left to the battleships *King George V* and *Rodney* approaching from the WNW. *Rodney* opened fire at 0847 followed by *King George V* at 0848 and within 15 minutes *Bismarck* (visible as smoke on the left of the picture) had lost half her main armament and all her fire control equipment. The British battleships, joined by the cruisers *Norfolk* and *Dorsetshire*, continued their pounding of *Bismarck* until 1021 when they ceased fire. [*IWM MH.15931*]

74. *Bismarck* on fire in the last stages of the action and visible as merely a column of smoke, photographed from one of the British warships. All her 38cm armament was out of action by 0931 and the rest of the action was little more than target practice. There was no hope for *Bismarck* so the order was given to set the scuttling charges and abandon ship.

75. The torpedo crew of the cruiser *Dorsetshire* which fired the final torpedoes that sank *Bismarck* (the hatching on the photograph is the mark of the censor). Despite the pounding his ships had given *Bismarck*, Admiral Tovey was still concerned that she could make port, so he decided to sink her by torpedo. *Dorsetshire* anticipated his instructions and at 1025 fired two torpedoes at a range of 3,600 yards into *Bismarck*'s starboard side. One exploded under the bridge while the other may have hit further aft. *Dorsetshire* then steamed round the battleship's bow and at 1036 fired another torpedo into her port side. At 1040 *Bismarck* was observed to turn over and sink in position 48°09′N, 16°07′W.

76. The lucky ones. Some of the 115 *Bismarck* survivors at a prisoner of war camp in Britain in June 1941. In time they would be shipped to other camps in Canada. [*IWM H.16895*]

77. An exhausted German seaman is hauled aboard the cruiser *Dorsetshire*, which rescued 85 survivors. The destroyer *Maori* picked up another 25 men in the heavy sea which was running, but in view of the possibility of German U-boats being in the area the rescue work was reluctantly abandoned. A further three survivors were found on a raft by *U.74*, while on 28 May the weather ship *Sachsenwald* found another two men. After an appeal from the German Government, the Spanish cruiser *Canarias* was sent to look for more survivors but found only wreckage and bodies. Thus only 115 out of *Bismarck*'s crew of over 2,200 officers and men were saved.

78

78. Burial of the dead. Off-duty men of the cruiser *Sheffield* muster on the quarterdeck on 28 May as Captain Larcom reads the burial service for Able Seaman Ling and Ordinary Seaman George. Twenty-four hours later Able Seaman Taylor was buried with equal ceremony. Apart from the loss of life in *Hood*, British casualties in the action were: two officers and twelve ratings killed and six ratings wounded in *Prince of Wales*; three killed and eight wounded in *Sheffield*; one rating killed in *Maori*; one rating washed overboard in *Sikh*; one officer and a rating wounded in *Zulu* and one officer and three ratings wounded in *Piorun* in air attacks following the sinking of *Bismarck*. [*IWM A.4103*]

79

79. 12 June 1941 saw the end of one of the many German supply ships in the Atlantic tasked with supporting raiders like *Bismarck*. The tanker *Friedrich Breme* burning after being set on fire by her crew after being caught by *Sheffield*. The cruiser was not deceived by *Breme*'s attempt to pass herself off as a Panamanian tanker bound for Land's End and a couple of rounds of 6in provided the inducement for the tanker's Master, Kapitän Schulze, to scuttle his ship. [*IWM A.4396*]

80. Rear Admiral W. F. Wake-Walker (photographed after being promoted to Vice-Admiral), Flag Officer commanding 1st Cruiser Squadron, whose shadowing work with *Norfolk* and *Suffolk* had done so much to bring about *Bismarck*'s destruction. Wake-Walker, with Captain Leach of *Prince of Wales*, was nearly a different sort of casualty of the *Bismarck* affair. Churchill wanted scapegoats for the failure to sink *Bismarck* sooner and trailed the idea of court-martialling Wake-Walker and Leach for breaking off the action with *Bismarck* after *Hood* had been sunk. Admiral Dudley Pound would have accepted Churchill's intervention were it not for the attitude taken by Admiral Tovey who, on hearing of the idea, threatened to haul down his flag and appear as the 'Prisoners' Friend'. No more was heard of this idea. [*IWM A.23581*]

Data Section

KM *Bismarck*: Design Particulars

Length:	792ft 4in (wl), 813ft 8in (oa)
Beam (max):	118ft 1in
Draught:	28ft 6in
Displacement:	41,700 tons standard, 50,900 tons full load
Deep draught:	34ft 9in (mean)

Machinery:
Three-shaft Brown-Boveri geared turbines, 12 Wagner superheated boilers: 163,000shp

Speed at load draught:	30 knots
Oil fuel at load draught:	3,388 tons
Oil fuel capacity:	7,900m³
Range at 15kt:	8,410nm

Armament:
Eight 38cm SK C/34 (4 × 2)
Twelve 15cm SK C/28 (6 × 2)

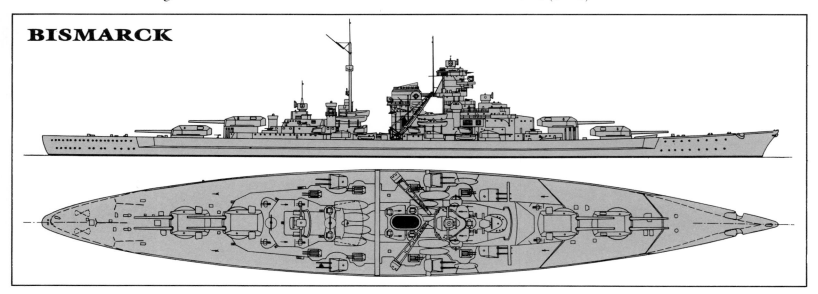

BISMARCK

Sixteen 10.5cm SK C/33 (8 × 2)
Sixteen 37mm SK C/30 (8 × 2)
Twelve 2cm machine-guns C/30 (12 × 1)
Six Arado Ar 196 aircraft, two catapults

Armour:

Belt:	12½–10½in
Deck:	2in
Armoured deck:	4¾–3in
Slopes:	4in
Torpedo bulkhead:	1¾in
38cm turrets:	14½–7in
15cm turrets:	4–1½in
Conning tower:	14–2in

Table of Weights (tons):

General Equipment:	1,445
Armament:	7,453
Armour:	17,256
Oil fuel:	3,388
Hull:	11,474
Machinery:	4,156
Total:	45,172
Ship's company:	2,092 officers and men

HMS *Hood*: final Legend (as approved on 30 August 1917)

Length:	810ft (oa), 860ft (pp)
Beam (max):	104ft
Draught:	28ft fwd, 29ft aft
Displacement:	41,200 tons
Deep draught:	31ft 6in (mean)

Machinery:

Four-shaft Brown Curtis geared turbines, 24 Yarrow boilers:	144,000shp

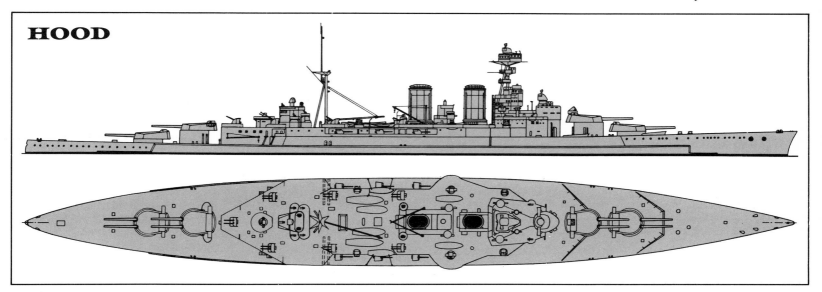

HOOD

Speed at load draught:	31 knots	
Oil fuel at load draught:	1,200 tons	
Oil fuel capacity:	4,000 tons	
Range at 10kt	4,000nm	

Armament:
Eight 15in 42 cal
Sixteen (later reduced to 12) 5.5in 50 cal
Four 4in HA
Two 21in submerged torpedo tubes
Eight (later reduced to 4) 21in above-water torpedo tubes

Armour:
Belt (amidships):	12in/7in/5in
Belt (forward):	6in/5in
Belt (aft):	6in
Bulkheads (fwd):	5in/4in
Bulkheads (aft):	5in/4in
Barbettes (max):	12in
Gunhouses:	15in front, 12in and 11in sides, 11in back and 5in roof

Conning tower:	11in, 10in, 9in and 7in. Conning tower tube 3in. Torpedo conning tower 6in
Vertical protective plating:	¾–1½in on bulkheads, 1½–2in on funnel uptakes
Horizontal protective plating:	1¼–2in on forecastle deck, ¾–2in on upper deck; and 3in on main deck. Lower deck (fwd) 1–1½in and 1–3in on lower deck aft

Table of Weights (tons):
General Equipment:	800
Armament:	5,255
Armour:	13,550
Oil fuel:	1,200
Hull:	14,950
Machinery:	3,500
Board Margin:	145
Total:	41,200

Ship's company:	1,477 officers and men